BODY ARMOR

EVERYTHING YOU NEED TO KNOW TO SURVIVE YOUR NEXT ENCOUNTER WITH THE POLICE

KEN REDFEARN

PAGE PUBLISHING, INC.
Conneaut Lake, PA

First originally published by
Page Publishing 2020

ISBN 978-1-64544-424-4 (pbk)
ISBN 978-1-64544-425-1 (digital)

Printed in the United States of America

In loving memory of
Barbara Redfearn.
May She Rest In Peace.

CONTENTS

INTRODUCTION

I remember being pulled over at the age of 17, by a white officer in Fairfax County, Virginia. He proceeded to walk around the vehicle and state, "Let's see what violations we can come up with today". He wrote a ticket for defected equipment, indicating one of the tires didn't have the sufficient amount of tread.

A year earlier, eight lanes of traffic was reduced to two lanes during rush hour. My cousin and I were stopped by six police cars. We were removed from the vehicle with force, by several officers, without probable cause. They then searched our persons and the vehicle without consent, only for them to release us after nothing illegal was found to justify an arrest.

This book includes information gathered from interviews conducted with current law enforcement officers from several different law enforcement agencies, with over 50 years of experience protecting the DC metropolitan and surrounding areas; and of course, my personal experience. In this book you will learn what to do when encountered by the police as a driver, passenger, pedestrian, and homeowner.

Feel free to use this as a quick reference tool to equip yourself with the knowledge needed on your rights, today's laws, and how they can help you survive your next encounter with the police.

You are encouraged to read twice!

DRIVER

1.1 Important Documents

I had the luxury to speak to several officers about where is the ideal location to store your important documents (license, vehicle registration, and proof of insurance). Although I received several different answers, including glove box and center console, all were concerned with the movement and placement of your hands when retrieving the documents.

A metropolitan police officer with seven years of experience suggested the sun visor.

The officer indicated the high visibility and thinness of the area poses less of a threat to an officer during a traffic stop.

Why is this so important? In Columbia, South Carolina, an unarmed black man, Levar Jones, was shot by a white State Trooper. Trooper Sean Groubert ordered Mr. Jones to retrieve his important documents, only to fire four times when he reached, striking Mr. Jones in the hip. Trooper Groubert was fired and charged. He pleaded guilty to assault and battery of a high and aggravated nature, and was sentenced to 12 years in prison, with 5 years suspended. Mr. Jones received a settlement of $285,000 from the State of South Carolina.

1.2 Being Pulled Over

When being pulled over by the police, find a safe place to stop. If you are on an interstate or highway, take the next exit. If one is not near, pull over as far to the right as possible, away from ongoing traffic.

It may be a good idea to retrieve your important documents once the officer arrives to your window, to avoid the appearance of suspicious movement. This is recommended by a veteran officer with experience in two different jurisdictions, in the State of Virginia.

By law, it is not required to roll your window completely down. In some places including the District of Columbia, you may be ordered to do so, if you have tinted windows that are obstructing the officer's view. Otherwise, it is not required as long as communication is clear, and the officer is able to obtain your important documents.

Ms. Victoria King, a 26-year-old black student at the University of Central Florida, filed an excessive force compliant. A campus police officer broke her window with his hands, and pulled her out the vehicle to arrest her for refusing to let her window completely down. The officer wanted Ms. King to sign a citation for one non-working brake light. Officer Timothy Issacs resigned from the force three years later. His resignation came in the mist of an independent investigation into his possible misconduct in a separate incident.

Once stopped, don't ask why you're being stopped immediately, allow the officer the opportunity to tell you. In Washington, D.C., it is part of the SOP (Standard Operating Procedure). This applies in most jurisdictions. Most officers will inform you shortly after approaching the vehicle; however, after turning over important documents, if not informed, you should ask.

I discovered, during this interview process, asking an officer why he or she pulled you over, could agitate them. Especially, if you didn't allow an adequate amount of time for them to inform you. This may not work for you in the long run; however, it is well within your rights. At any point during a traffic stop, if you become uncomfortable, you have the right to request a supervisor to the scene.

1.3 Suspended/Revoked License

According to a Corporal with 10 years of experience with the Prince Georges County Police Department, operating a motor vehicle with a suspended/revoked or without a permit, will result in a citation, but not necessarily an arrest. If you have an invalid registration, insurance card, or driver's license, it will result in an automatic citation, even if all the current information is the same.

Officers I spoke with in the State of Maryland indicated, there are certain circumstances in which you may be allowed to drive away from the scene without a license. For example, if you have a small child in the vehicle, if you have a serious emergency, or if you live nearby. If you have a licensed driver, as a passenger, the officer may allow that individual to drive. If not, the officer can order the vehicle parked and allow you to walk away from the scene. If your vehicle isn't properly registered and/or insured, it most likely will be towed. Please keep in mind that most of these decisions are at the officer's discretion.

SECTION 1

If you are driving without a license or it's suspended/revoked, hopefully you are touring the historic City of Williamsburg, Virginia. According to a four year veteran of the James City County Police Department, not being properly licensed would most likely *never* result in an arrest. In the party city of Virginia Beach, driving without knowledge of a revoked/suspended license will not result in an initial arrest, but will any stop thereafter.

All officers I spoke with in Washington D.C., agreed that operating a vehicle without a valid permit will result in an automatic arrest.

I guess God was with me years ago, that summer night. I was awakened by a screaming alarm clock indicating 1:45 am, 15 minutes away from the start of my 2:00 am air shift. Late as hell, I took off down a N.E. Washington D.C. street at a high rate of speed. After blowing through a few stop signs and a red light at Hawaii Avenue, I noticed a police car in my rear view mirror closing in; sirens blazing! The two officers approached from opposite sides of the vehicle. The elder white gentleman asked, "How many were you going to run?". He returned to his vehicle with my license and registration, at which time I confided in the younger African American officer. I informed him of my current suspended driving status, and my work dilemma. He suggested that I "be honest" with the other officer, indicating he was a fair guy. The other officer returned, aware of my suspended permit. I explained to him that I was a radio personality, currently late for an on-air shift. With some hesitation, displaying doubt, he ordered me to call the current jock on-air. K-Man. explained to the officer, not only was I telling the truth, but he was unable to leave until my arrival. At which time I was released, without even a ticket.

In the State of South Carolina, 50-year-old Walter Scott decided not to leave his fate in the officer's hands, and chose to run. He was pulled over for one non-functioning brake light, at which time the officer discovered the vehicle wasn't properly registered.

Mr. Scott, father of four, had an outstanding warrant for back child support payments. A white North Charleston police officer, 1st Class Michael Slager, pursued Mr. Scott a short distance before discharging his service weapon several times, striking the former member of the U.S. Coast Guard five times as he fled. Officer Slager, who lied to dispatch and said Mr. Scott went for his taser, was sentenced to 20 years in federal prison. He pleaded guilty to violation of civil rights, by acting under the color of law. Mr. Scott's family was awarded $6.5 million.

Fleeing the scene on foot is a misdemeanor in most jurisdictions.

1.4 Eluding and Fleeing

As a driver, it's important to know the U.S. Supreme Court on June 9, 2011, ruled in an Indiana case, Sykes vs. United States; "fleeing" in a vehicle is a violent felony. The Court said in part, "When a perpetrator flees police in a car, his determination to elude capture makes a lack of concern for the safety of others". In South Carolina, the penalty for failure to stop for a blue light is 90 days to 3 years imprisonment, if no death or serious injury occurs. More information on fleeing and eluding in Pedestrian 3.2.

1.5 Being Asked to Exit the Vehicle

By all means, you want to remain in your vehicle during a traffic stop. A 12-year veteran with the Metropolitan Police Department, stated that in the District of Columbia, its preferred that you remain in your vehicle. A Corporal in the Prince George's County Police Department, with over a decade of experience said, if asked to exit the vehicle in the State of Maryland, tell the officer you feel safer in the vehicle. An officer with experience in more than one jurisdiction in the State of Virginia, said in the Commonwealth, an officer has the right to order you out the vehicle, at their discretion.

A police officer with the City of Alexandria Police Department, with 24 years of experience in law enforcement, disagrees.

This may seem somewhat confusing. What I've learned during the course of this research is many officers have different interpretations of the law, even in the same state. This is why it is so important to question an officer who may be in violation of your rights, but I advise you to comply, <u>if your life does not depend on it</u>. This will preserve your right to contest later.

There are certain situations in which the officer has the right to order you to exit the vehicle.

1. If any of your important documents are not valid or present.
2. Something illegal is in "plain sight".
3. The smell of marijuana (except in Washington, D.C.) or any other illegal narcotic.
4. If the officer feels you are driving under the influence or intoxicated.
5. You and/or your vehicle fits the description of a suspect or vehicle that is wanted in connection to a

crime, making you the subject of an investigation.

6. If you're being placed under arrest.

In many states, including Maryland, Virginia, and in the District of Columbia, this would be considered "probable cause".

WHAT IS PROBABLE CAUSE: Probable Cause is when a prudent officer has beyond reasonable doubt (facts and/or evidence) that a crime has been committed by the confronted individual. When an officer believes someone has committed a crime or is about to committed a crime, based on factual evidence and/or circumstances.

None of the above applied in Waller County, Texas, when State Trooper, Brian Encinia, bucked a u-turn and began to trail a 28-year-old Prairie View A&M graduate. He stopped the young African American woman for failure to signal when she switched lanes, to allow the pursing officer to pass. State Trooper Encinia clearly lost his cool, when he ordered Sandra Bland out of her vehicle without probable cause. Trooper Encinia became agitated with Ms. Bland's refusal to extinguish her cigarette, in which she didn't have to. Ms. Bland was handled aggressively during the arrest process. Most of the interaction was not caught on film because the officer was not wearing a bodycam. He appeared to intentionally move Ms. Bland from the view of the police car's dash camera.

If you are removed from the vehicle, try to remain in front of the dash cam, even if the officer is wearing a bodycam; the footage from the dash cam cannot be turned off. Ms. Bland, a native of Chicago, was in town to take a job at her Alma mater. She never had her day in court. She was found dead in her jail cell three days later.

Trooper Encinia was fired, and charged with perjury for lying about why Ms. Bland was removed from her vehicle. Charges were dropped after an agreement was reached with the Waller County Prosecutor, which included to never pursue a career in law enforcement again. The Bland Family was against the charges being dropped. They were awarded $1.9 million in a wrongful death lawsuit.

Remember, it's best to comply, but you have the right to ask questions.

1.6 Police Search

A 28 year veteran with the Washington, D.C. Metropolitan Police Department said, "By law, you have the expectation of privacy in your vehicle". Never give consent to have your vehicle searched!

An officer can not conduct a search, unless:

1. **YOU** give consent!
2. He or she has a search warrant.
3. Something illegal is in "plain sight".
4. There is a smell of marijuana (except in Washington, D.C.) or other narcotics.
5. Detection of the presence of narcotics, by a trained K9.
6. You're being arrested.

SECTION 1

Keep in mind, a "pat down" and "search" are two different things. A "pat down" is conducted for an officer's safety and yours. It is a patting or rubbing of your outermost garments. This is a check for weapons only. An officer may squeeze your pockets, but legally, can not go into your pockets. He or she may ask you for permission to enter your pocket(s), ask you to remove the contents, or ask for a description of the contents, in which you do **not** have to comply. An officer may use several tactics to try to convince you to consent to a search. No matter what, the answer should always be NO. In most situations, the officer has the right to conduct a pat down.

In Washington, D.C., the smell of marijuana is not grounds to search your vehicle. You can carry up to two ounces legally. In Maryland, Virginia, and many other jurisdictions, it would be probable cause for a search. Most likely, you will only be issued a citation in those states, if you are in possession of a small amount. For example, in the State of

Maryland, if you have 10 grams or less, you will be fined $100-$500.

Currently under Virginia Law Section 18.2-250.1, possession of marijuana is a misdemeanor. It is punishable by a fine up to $500 and/or up to 30 days in jail. Many prominent Virginia politicians have been in favor of the decriminalization and legalization of marijuana, including Governor Mark Northam and Lieutenant Governor Justin Fairfax.

On June 15, 2019, Virginia Attorney General Mark Herring stated to a group of reporters, "We are needlessly creating criminals and getting a lot of convictions… And this whole system—the weight of it—falls disproportionately on African Americans and people of color. There is a better, smarter way to approach cannabis, and it starts with decriminalizing simple possession of small amounts, addressing past convictions and moving thoughtfully toward legal and regulated adult use."

SECTION 1

In November, Democrats won majority control of both legislative chambers in the Virginia House of Delegates.

Weeks later, Senator Adam Ebbin pre-filed a bill for 2020 session to decriminalize the possession of marijuana. Ebbin proposed making up to an ounce of cannabis punishable by a maximum $50 civil penalty.

Decriminalization and legalization has been echoed by many lawmakers in Virginia. Decriminalization was a campaign promise of Governor Ralph Northam.

On December 11, 2019, the newly formed cannabis caucus and other lawmakers met at the Virginia Cannabis Summit to discuss different proposals. They also heard from officials from different states where legalization has already occurred.

Laws vary by state, please check the laws in your jurisdiction, online, or at your local library.

If you are asked by an officer to allow a "search", respectfully decline.

1.7 Driving Under the Influence (DUI)/Driving While Intoxicated (DWI)

Driving while intoxicated or under the influence is a serious offense. You may be surprised to know, its a misdemeanor in most states, unless you are a repeat offender. The legal blood alcohol limit is 0.08%. You can be arrested with a lower blood alcohol level, if the officer feels you are displaying signs of impairment. More than one DUI/DWI could result in a felony charge.

In some jurisdictions, including the State of Virginia, refusal to consent to a breathalyzer will result in an automatic arrest and suspension of your driver's license. The hand-held breathalyzer is used by an officer to determine your level of intoxication, but is not admissible in court. If placed under arrest, there is a second breathalyzer at the police station, in which you must take.

One common mistake is for a driver to sit behind the wheel while intoxicated. If you are in the driver's seat, you can be charged with DUI/DWI, even if the vehicle is not in motion. In order to prevent this, move from behind the wheel (driver's seat) to a passenger seat, preferably, the backseat. This will allow you to avoid arrest, if you need more time to rest or sober up.

If you make the decision to pull over while intoxicated, please be sure to choose a safe location (off street, in a well-lit area). I strongly encourage you NOT to pull over to the side of a major highway or street, with continuous traffic. Not only could this be dangerous, but could result in an arrest, if the officer determines you drove to that location.

DUI/DWI cannot be expunged from your record, due to the Mothers Against Drunk Driving Initiative.

27-year-old George Wingate was arrested, despite not being under the influence. Mr. Wingate pulled to the side of the road after experiencing car trouble. Dash cam caught Mr. Wingate asking Stafford County Sheriff's Deputy S.A. Fulford several times if he was being detained, in which the Deputy replied "no", but denied him the right to leave the scene. Mr. Wingate was placed under arrest after refusing to show identification.

By law in many states, including Virginia and in the District of Columbia, this is considered consensual contact. Mr. Wingate wasn't the subject of an investigation; therefore, he was not required to present identification, and should have been able to leave the scene at his discretion. Mr. Wingate was charged with failure to show identification, obstruction of justice, and resisting arrest. All charges were eventually dropped. Mr. Wingate filed a federal lawsuit against Deputy S.A. Fulford under the grounds that his Fourth Amendment rights were violated. More on the Fourth Amendment, in Pedestrian 3.3.

1.8 Detained / Miranda Rights

Being detained does not necessarily mean you are under arrest, even if you are handcuffed and/or placed in a police vehicle.

Reasons why an officer may detain you:

1. To control the scene or the situation.
2. The appearance of something illegal is in "plain sight".
3. You are suspected in a crime and/or a crime is being investigated.
4. If an officer thinks you may run.
5. You are a threat to yourself or others.
6. You are being placed under arrest.

If arrested, its very important to remain silent. This is one of your four rights/warnings, in which an officer must state to you, prior to questioning.

1. You have the right to remain silent.

2. Anything you say can, and will be used against you, in a court of law.
3. You have the right to an attorney during questioning.
4. If you cannot afford an attorney, one will be appointed to you.

Theses are known as your Miranda Rights. In 1966, the U.S. Supreme Court ruled 5-4 in favor of Ernesto Miranda, who was convicted after a two-hour interrogation without counsel, yielded a confession. The highest court ruled, the confession could not be introduced as evidence in the trial, because the police failed to inform Mr. Miranda of his rights to have an attorney and against self-incrimination. These warnings must be given by the police as stated in the Fifth Amendment, "you have the right not to be a witness against yourself", and the Sixth Amendment, "you have the right to an attorney".

Keep in mind, once your Miranda Rights are read to you, an officer will immediately begin to ask you questions. You should inform the officer that you wish to remain silent. If an officer fails to read you your Miranda Rights, anything said is **not** admissible in court.

You should have an attorney present during questioning. If you decide to answer questions without one, which isn't advised, you have the right to end the conversation at any time.

If you see an emergency vehicle on the side of the road (police, ambulance, fire truck, etc.), in some jurisdictions, including the State of Maryland and Virginia, it is required that you put a lane between your vehicle and the emergency vehicle. This offense is only enforced if you can do so safely. Failure to do so, is punishable by a citation. If you are unable to get over, it is lawful to maintain your lane, at a reduce rate of speed. The State of Maryland Move Over Law expanded, effective October 1, 2018, to include service vehicles, tow trucks, construction vehicles, and construction equipment. Violators of this law face fines up to $750, and 3 points on your driving record.

PASSENGER

2.1 Responsibilities

In this section, you will learn not only your rights as a passenger, but your responsibilities, as well. Before I get to your rights, let's cover your responsibilities as a passenger. Some may find this corny, but this is a very important tool in the guide to survival.

First, know who you are riding with. Is the individual wanted by the law? Do they have a suspended or revoked license, or not licensed at all? Second, is there anything illegal in the vehicle (drugs, guns, prescription drugs without labels, etc.)? Third, check the windshield and license plate for current/valid stickers and decals. This should give you an indication if the vehicle is legally registered. It's also a good idea to ask the driver if they have their important documents (driver's license, vehicle registration, and proof of insurance). Make sure all documents are onboard, and in an easy to reach location. None of this matters if the vehicle is stolen or used without authorization.

2.2 Being Pulled Over

When being pulled over as a passenger, in most jurisdictions, the officer's main concern is the driver. If the vehicle or the driver fits a description of one being involved in a crime, you could be the subject of an investigation. Being part of an investigation would give the officer probable cause to ask for your identification; however, if the vehicle was stopped for a traffic violation, such as speeding, improper lane change, etc., you are not required to identify yourself or provide identification. Be aware the officer may ask you to identify yourself anyway; but by law, you do not have to comply.

2.3 Contact

As a passenger in a vehicle, who is not the subject of an investigation, your communication with the officer would be considered consensual contact. By law, you are not required to provide identification. Communication can begin and end, at your discretion.

Showing your identification may be necessary in certain situations. For example, if the driver is driving on suspended/revoked license or is under the influence. If you are a licensed driver, the officer may allow you to drive the vehicle away.

2.4 Being Asked to Exit the Vehicle

Most of the officers I spoke with said, they are not interested in the passenger(s) getting out the vehicle.

Listed below are a few reasons, in which an officer may ask you to get out the vehicle:

1. Subject of an Investigation
2. Fruits of a Crime—Officer sees item(s) that could be related to an incident or crime under investigation.
3. The smell of marijuana (except for in Washington, D.C.) or other narcotics.
4. If the Officer observes excessive movements from the passenger(s) during the execution of the traffic stop.

If you are asked to get out of the vehicle, as a passenger, politely ask the officer why is it necessary.

2.5 Police Search

As covered under Driver 1.5, unless there is something in plain sight, the smell of marijuana (except in Washington, D.C.), the odor of another narcotic, or you are the subject of a criminal investigation, the officer does not have the right to search the passenger by law; only a pat down.

In Washington D.C., a passenger is allowed to possess up to two ounces of marijuana legally.

2.6 Intoxication

As stated in Passenger 2.1, most officers are not concerned with the passenger(s) during a traffic stop, even if he or she is under the influence. Unless you are being disruptive, confrontational or impeding the officer's ability to perform his or her duty. Under those circumstances, you could be arrested for public intoxication and/or obstruction of justice. You should never be asked to take a breathalyzer, as a passenger. You should never consent to a breathalyzer, unless it's necessary for an officer to check your ability to drive the vehicle.

2.7 Being Detained

As a passenger in a vehicle that has been pulled over by the police, according to several officers in most jurisdictions, everyone in the vehicle (driver and all passengers), are detained. You cannot exit the vehicle even though you are not the driver. If it's only a traffic violation or a criminal investigation not involving you, you can seek permission from the officer to leave the scene immediately.

One summer night, as a teen, I was a passenger in a vehicle, with a group of friends. We were pulled over by the police. The officer along with a partner, asked all of us for identification, one by one. By the time the officer reached me, he had already obtained identification from three of us. By this time, it had been determined that the driver's permit was suspended. The officer asked me for my identification, I asked, "Why?". He repeated himself with an aggressive tone, and I asked "Why?" again. He replied that he was trying to see if anyone could drive the vehicle away from the scene. I replied, "I cannot", and asked if I was being detained. In which he replied, "Go! You want to leave? Go!", and then the rest of my friends proceeded to ask if they were being detained.

In most situations if the stop is only traffic related, an officer will allow you, as the passenger, to leave the scene, on foot, if you choose to. (As long as the stop occurs in a location, in which it's safe for you to walk away.)

PEDESTRIAN

3.1 Contact

As a pedestrian, if you are walking along minding your own business, you do not have to comply to contact with an officer. The Officer must inform you that you're being detained, or is the subject of an investigation. In Washington D.C., there is an old law on the books, requiring you to identify yourself to an officer. According to a veteran on the police force, you can state your name without showing identification, and continue on your way. You are not required to answer any questions.

One of the main reasons I suggest you comply to an officer's request, without forfeiting your rights, is to avoid an officer from taking the law into their own hands. The video went viral, of 26 year old Deshawn McGrier being repeatedly punched in the face by Officer Arthur Williams, with the City of Baltimore Police Department. Mr. McGrier was being punched in the face for refusing to provide identification, in which he did not have to. Officer Williams continued to punch Mr. McGrier after he fell to the ground, breaking his jaw, nose, and ribs. Officer Williams clearly already knew Mr. McGrier's identity from an arrest made just weeks earlier.

Baltimore Police Commissioner Gary Tuggle said at a press conference, the incident could be proof that police training may be lacking, citing the need for more "scenario-based" training and less "pen-and-pencil" lectures. "Neither of us can say why this happened. If it were borne out of emotion, we're trained—we should be trained to never act in an emotional way, particularly when it comes to engaging with citizens... The situation shows us another deficiency in our training that we can learn from."

Officer Williams resigned after being suspended. He was charged with one felony assault, one misdemeanor assault, and a misdemeanor count of misconduct in office, according to State's Attorney Marilyn Mosley.

3.2 Fleeing/Eluding

Fleeing/eluding (running) from the scene does not constitute probable cause for a chase, search, and/or detainment. You must make physical contact with an officer or be the subject of an investigation. If an officer has <u>not</u> informed you that you are being detained, due to an investigation, you have the right to leave the scene at your discretion. This can be in the form of running or walking. If you decide to flee, and is apprehended by an officer, you have not forfeited any of your rights.

Although the City of Baltimore Police Department tried to justify the arrest of Freddie Gray, by saying he was carrying an illegal knife; the pursuit itself was not legal.

City State's Attorney Marilyn Mosby stated, "Lieutenant [Brian W.] Rice, Officer [Garrett E.] Miller, and Officer [Edward M.] Nero failed to establish probable cause for Mr. Gray's arrest, as no crime had been committed by Mr. Gray," Mosby said. "Accordingly, Lieutenant Rice, Officer Miller, and Officer Nero illegally arrested Mr. Gray."

The trio, led by Lieutenant Rice, chased Freddie Gray. The Lieutenant claims Freddie Gray and another individual fled the scene at North Avenue and Mount Street, after making eye contact with him. This was disputed by Deputy State's Attorney Janice Bledsoe.

Mr. Gray surrendered when he came in contact with the pursuing officers. He stated to the officers he could not breathe, and requested his inhaler. Mr. Gray was placed in the back of a transport van, but not buckled. Ceasar R. Goodson Jr., one of the six officers charged with the death of Freddie Gray, was the driver. He reportedly became agitated with Mr. Gray, and pulled over to place him in leg restraints, despite his repeated request for medical attention.

Officer Porter, another one of the six officers charged, arrived at one of the many stops made by Officer Goodson. He came to conduct a welfare check on Mr. Gray, at Goodson's request. Officer Porter reportedly helped Mr. Gray, who was never buckled, off the floor of the van. Mr. Gray repeated his request for medical attention. The officers were distracted by dispatch, ordering yet another stop for the van. Consequentially, medical attention was not sought for Freddie Gray until his arrival at the District House police station, nearly 45 minutes after his initial request.

ABC local news affiliate WJLA, reported Freddie Gray, who sustained a broken neck, had a dent in the back of his head that matched the bolt inside the rear of the van. Goodson was charged with murder; the prosecution believed he intentionally gave Mr. Gray a "rough ride".

Freddie Gray died a week later from his injuries. All six officers were acquitted in the death of Mr. Gray, despite the fact that he suffered a broken spine in police custody. Baltimore City Police Department admitted to making errors, including failure to secure Mr. Gray in the police van, and failure to grant medical attention when requested. The Gray family received a settlement of $6.4 million in a wrongful death lawsuit.

3.3 Police Search

As covered in Driver 1.5, an officer must have a warrant or your consent to search you, unless you are being placed under arrest or is the subject of an investigation, involving a crime. Be aware of an officer's attempt to convince or manipulate you into consenting to a search. During a check for weapons, he or she may squeeze your pockets and ask for a description of the contents. The officer may ask you to empty your pockets, or even boldly ask for permission to remove the contents of your pockets; all of which by law, you have the right to say "no". If questioned about the contents of your pockets during a "pat down" for weapons, you can name the items if you choose to. It would be considered lawful to reply, "not a weapon".

The Fourth Amendment protects your rights from unreasonable intrusions by the government. However, it does not guarantee protection from all searches and seizures, but only those done by the government and deemed unreasonable under the law. The Fourth Amendment of the U.S. Constitution, states "the right of the people to be secure in their persons, houses, papers, and effects, against unreasonable searches and seizures, shall not be violated, and no Warrants shall issue, but upon probable cause, supported by Oath or affirmation, and particularly describing the place to be searched, and the persons or things to be seized."

3.4 Intoxication

Unless you are operating a motor vehicle, you will almost never be subjected to taking a breathalyzer, according to several police officers. In most jurisdictions, there is a charge on the books for public intoxication. Public intoxication is usually only initiated by an officer in which a subject is being combative, unruly or noncompliant. It's usually assessed incorporation with others charges or when an officer has nothing else to charge you with, and it's obvious you have been drinking. In others words, a happy drunk pedestrian, who is compliant, is usually allowed to proceed on his or her way.

3.5 Detained/Arrested

The only time you should be detained as a pedestrian, is if you are the subject of an investigation or if you are being placed under arrest. As covered in Driver 1.7, being handcuffed or placed in a police vehicle, does not necessarily mean you are being placed under arrest. Refer to Driver 1.7, as a refresher on various reasons why you may be detained.

If you are being placed under arrest, the most important thing to remember is your right to remain silent. As stated by the arresting officer, everything you say, can and will be used against you.

As stated in Driver 1.4, it is very important to stay in the view of the dash cam, if possible. This is key during an encounter of any kind with the police, whether you are a driver, passenger, or pedestrian. On the Southside of Chicago, eight officers faced charges after a dash cam video revealed a cover up in the death of Laquan McDonald, who was shot 16 times by Officer Jason Van Dyke. Officer Van Dyke discharged his service weapon within six seconds of arriving on the scene. According to Officer Van Dyke, he was in fear for his life when he fired while stepping backwards, away from the teen brandishing a knife, claiming he lunged towards him.

This was also supported by other officers, but totally refuted by the dash cam footage. The footage showed Officer Van Dyke firing from at least 10 feet away while moving forward, as the teen walked away. Nine of the sixteen bullets struck the 17-year-old in his back. Officer Jason Van Dyke continued to fire up to 13 seconds after the teen was on the ground. He was charged 13 months later, just hours before the release of the video, after the prosecution lost a long battle to keep the footage sealed.

Laquan McDonald was the subject of an investigation into auto break-ins at a trucking yard before the shooting occurred. Dispatch was requesting a unit with a taser, because officers on the scene believed the teenager was under the influence of Phencyclidine (PCP), also known as angel dust, love boat, dipper, among other names. It is a drug used for its mind-altering effects. PCP may cause hallucinations, distorted perceptions of sounds, and violent behavior.

The McDonald Family was awarded $5 million seven months after the shooting, despite never filing a wrongful death lawsuit against the City of Chicago. On October 5, 2018, Officer Jason Van Dyke became the first police officer to be convicted of first-degree murder since 1980. The other officers were acquitted of all charges.

HOMEOWNERS

4.1 Domestic Dispute

A domestic dispute is the number one reason why an officer would be called to your home. If the police are called to your home for a domestic dispute, and you are not the caller, the officer will insist on speaking to the caller upon their arrival, as a welfare check. This is one of the few situations, in which ignoring the knock at the door will not work.

If the person has sustained visible injuries, you will be arrested. In some jurisdictions, including Washington D.C., you will be required to spend the night in jail, as a "cooling off period". If both parties are displaying injuries, both are subject to arrest.

Domestic violence in the District of Columbia is labeled as an intrafamily offense. Applicable to any interpersonal, intimate, partner, or family violence.

Types of domestic violence:

Interpersonal violence—is a criminal act committed by an offender upon a person with whom the offender shares or has shared residence.

Intimate partner violence—is a criminal act committed by an offender upon a person to whom the offender is or was married. With whom the offender is or was in a domestic partnership or was in a romantic relationship.

Intrafamily violence—is a criminal act committed by an offender upon a person to whom the offender is related by blood, adoption, legal custody, marriage or domestic partnership or with whom the offender has a child in common.

The State of Maryland defines domestic violence "abuse", as the occurrence of one or more of the following acts between "family or household members":

- Assault
- An act that places a person in fear of imminent serious bodily harm
- An act that causes serious bodily harm
- Rape or sexual offense
- Attempt rape or sexual offense
- Stalking
- False imprisonment, such as interference with freedom, physically keeping you from leaving your home or kidnapping you.

In the State of Virginia, domestic violence may be considered a civil or criminal matter.

- Civil matters include those when a party is seeking a Protective Order, ordering another person to stop certain actions.
- Criminal matters of domestic assault and battery is when the perpetrator of the violence may be jailed or ordered to comply with various conditions if the defendant is found guilty.

Believe it or not, police shoot white people too! In Springfield, Virginia, John Geer was shot and killed standing in the doorway of his home. Fairfax County Police Officer Adam Torres, fired a single shot striking the unarmed 46-year-old, after a 42 minute standoff. Officer Torres claimed Mr. Geer's hands (which were above his head) dropped rapidly to his waist; however, other officers and witnesses on the scene, said his hands "remained above his shoulders". Mr. Geer informed the police officers upon their arrival, he had a gun, because they had guns too. Mr. Geer placed the holstered gun on the ground, at his feet, and never reached for it again.

Officer Adam Torres was one of the first two officers to the scene. Police were called to the home for a domestic situation. John Geer was upset and intoxicated, because his wife informed him that she was leaving him. Mr. Geer accidentally struck his daughter while tossing a suitcase. She dialed 911, and told dispatch he was throwing things. Mr. Geer's family was awarded nearly $3 million. Officer Torres who was fired and charged, plead guilty to involuntary man slaughter, and was sentenced to one year in jail. With time served, he was released five days after sentencing. Former Officer Torres was the first Fairfax County Police Officer to be convicted of an on-duty shooting.

If it isn't a domestic violence call, or a situation in which an officer feels that someone inside is in need of help or medical attention, you can ignore the police at the door. If you choose to answer your door, the officer(s) cannot enter your home without your consent, and you can end the conversation at your discretion.

4.2 Knock at the Door

In addition to a domestic violence situation, another reason why you may receive a knock at the door by the police, is if you are in violation of the noise ordinance. In the District of Columbia, between the hours of 10pm to 7am, noise must be kept at 55 decibels or below, and 60 decibels during the day, between the hours of 7am to 10pm, in a residential area. 55 decibels is the equivalent of a normal conversation, such as in a restaurant, office or quiet suburb. Violators are subject to a $500 fine, and/or up to 90 days in jail. In the States of Maryland and Virginia, noise ordinance vary by County. Check the laws in your local area to be informed.

4.3 Warrants (Searches)

If you, a member of your household, or a guest, has a warrant for arrest, you will receive a knock at the door. This does not give the police permission to search or even enter your home. If you are not the individual wanted, the police will need your consent to search your home for that individual. Keep in mind, police will try several tactics to convince you to consent (including threatening you with charges), but by law, you can say "no".

A search warrant, signed by a judge, gives an officer the right to search your home for specific items with or without your permission. Such a warrant may be served prior to the search or a "No Knock Warrant" may be conducted for the element of surprise, to protect law enforcement, in which case the entrance will be breached. The officer will yell "search warrant", while forcing entry. Of course, your rights are protected against illegal searches, as stated in the Fourth Amendment, covered in Pedestrian 3.3.

4.4 Guests

If you are the homeowner or are in legal possession of a property, you may ask the guest to leave at any time, even if you have granted initial permission to enter. You can call the police to assist you in getting an unwanted guest to leave, if that guest refuses to leave once the request has been made by the police officer, he or she can be arrested for trespassing.

You have to be careful with overnight guests, because getting them to leave can be tricky. In many jurisdictions, the matter would not be considered criminal, but civil.

According to the Maryland Law Library, if a guest or squatter refuses to leave, you may seek eviction by filing a "wrongful detainer" action in District Court. "Wrongful detainer" means to hold possession of real property (house, apartment, building, land) without the right of possession. You may not use "wrongful detainer" to evict current or holding-over tenants. You also may not use it for someone who has possession of the property by court order. Eviction is a legal procedure. As a landlord, in order to evict a tenant, you must seek a judgement through the District Court, until then, it would be unlawful to kick out the tenant, remove any of their belongings, turn off utilities or change the locks.

Reasons in which you can evict a tenant:

1. Nonpayment of Rent—As a landlord, you can begin the eviction process as soon as your rent due date has passed.
2. "Holding over"—If your tenant does not move out at the end of the lease, you may evict for "holding over", but in order to do this, tenant must receive proper written notice (at least one month) of the ending of the lease.
3. Breach of Lease—As a landlord, you may evict your tenant for breaking the terms of the lease. You must give at least 30 days advance written notice ending the lease, unless the tenant has exhibited behavior that constitutes a threat to others' safety, in which case, only a 14-day notice is required.

In the District of Columbia, a guest could be considered a tenant, if an agreement to pay rent has been reached with the homeowner (verbal or written), to pay rent through cash or labor, even if the agreement hasn't been fulfilled in anyway. With or without an agreement in place, in order to evict a guest, you have to file an eviction case in the Landlord And Tenant Branch in DC Superior Court.

In the State of Virginia, a guest is considered a month-to-month tenant without an agreement in place (written or verbal); therefore, a 30-day "Notice of Termination" must be issued in writing, in order to start the eviction process.

Please keep in mind that police are powerless in these civil matters, and should not be called. It could result in an unfavorable situation, if you're charged with a crime, such as "Disturbing the Peace", "Disorderly Conduct", etc.

SECTION 5

*BONUS SECTION—
CONCEALED WEAPONS

In the State of Maryland, you must apply for a Concealed Carry Weapon Permit (CCW). You are required to have a good reason in order to carry a firearm. If you are a law enforcement officer (current or retired), security guard, business owner, or if your life has been threatened, you will most likely be granted approval. Outside of law enforcement, if you are granted the right to carry a firearm, it is unlawful to conceal; it must be visible at all times.

A gun law took affect as of October 1, 2018, requiring any gun owners convicted of domestic violence to surrender their firearm. As part of the law, a judge can order the seizure of a gun owner's firearm, if the family deems them unstable.

Out-of-state CCW Permit Holders traveling through the State of Maryland should be aware, your firearm must be kept in a locked container, separate from ammunition, and out of reach. Maryland gun owners without a CCW Permit, must store their firearm in the same manner, while in transit. The possession would be considered lawful, traveling to and from the gun range.

In Washington, D.C., it is lawful to carry a firearm on your person, if you have a Concealed Carry Weapon Permit (CCW) issued by the District of Columbia, or a state in which reciprocity applies. The weapon must remain concealed and on your person unless in transit, in which it must be unloaded and stored in a locked container.

Also in Washington, D.C., you are required to inform an officer that you are in possession of your firearm, after you are greeted. I was told failure to do so, is not a crime. The officer has the right to confirm you are a permit holder, and your firearm is legally registered. By law, you are allowed to carry enough rounds to fill your weapon and to reload, totaling, but not exceeding 20 rounds. In other words, it is unlawful to carry a weapon that fires more than 10 rounds. At the same time, if you have a six shot revolver, it would be unlawful to be in possession of 13 bullets. With that said, there is no limit to the number of registered guns you can have, on your person or in your home.

You do not have to be a resident of the State of Virginia or Washington, D.C., in order to obtain a CCW Permit in those jurisdictions and many others. Washington, D.C. requires you to be in possession of a CCW permit from another state in order to obtain one, if you are not a resident.

The Commonwealth of Virginia, is an open carry state. You can lawfully carry a gun on your person or in your vehicle, with or without a permit. In your vehicle, the firearm must be in a secured container, such as glove box or center console. The container does not have to be locked.

If the firearm is on your person, it must be visible, unless you have a Concealed Carry Weapon Permit, issued by any state in which reciprocity applies. A Law Enforcement Officer in the State of Virginia, said, if informed that a CCW Permit holder is in possession of a firearm during a traffic stop, they would only instruct the occupant(s) of the vehicle not to reach for the weapon. By law you are not obligated to inform the officer.

Things clearly escalated quickly in St. Paul, Minnesota, when 32-year-old Philando Castillo was shot five times. He was complying with an officer's request for his important documents, during a traffic stop for a non working brake light. Mr. Castillo, while obtaining his driver's license, informed the officer that he was a CCW Permit holder, and was in possession of his firearm. St. Anthony County Police Officer Jeronimo Yanez screamed, "Don't pull it out!", before discharging his service weapon seven times. Mr. Castillo could be heard saying "I'm not", prior to the sounds of shots ringing out, in which he repeated after being struck. Two of the rounds pierced his heart. Several minutes of the incident played out live on Facebook, posted by his girlfriend, Diamond Reynolds. Ms. Reynolds was a passenger in the vehicle at the time of the shooting, along with her 4-year old daughter.

Ms. Reynolds received a settlement totaling $800,000 for emotional distress. The Castillo family received $2.9 million in a wrongful death settlement. Officer Yanez was fired from the Department; however, was acquitted on second-degree manslaughter charges.

A current veteran officer with the Metropolitan Police Department stated whenever pulled over by the police, he does not inform the officer he is in possession of a firearm. This could make an officer nervous; however, he believes it is necessary if you are complying with an officer's request to exit the vehicle.

It is very important to remember you are the only one who knows you are a CCW Permit holder. Whether you are defending yourself or others, remember you appear to most as an individual with a gun. Which means to many, you are the bad guy or girl. If you are in a situation in which you have to draw your firearm, you should attempt to notify others that you are a CCW Permit holder. I'm even in favor of shouting it out loud repeatedly, if it will not compromise your safety. Even police officers yell out "Blue... Blue... Blue!", as a warning, when entering each other's line of fire.

Emantic Bradford Jr., known as "EJ", enlisted in the Armed Forces to serve his country. On Thanksgiving night 2018, according to a witness, Mr. Bradford went from "shopper" to "Shepard" of frightened people, as shots rung out at the Riverchase Galleria. The Galleria is the largest mall in Alabama, located in Hoover (just outside of Birmingham). Bradford, a CCW Permit holder, put his hand on his firearm, as people scrambled for safety. Survivor, Ashlyn McMillan, called Mr. Bradford a "hero" for instructing her, and others to get down and to get into the store. The 20-year-old was mistaken as the mall shooter, and was shot 3 times from behind by an unnamed Hoover Officer working at the mall. Police initially named Mr. Bradford as the mall shooter, but corrected themselves a day later. The real suspect was later arrested, and charged with attempted murder of the 18-year old victim shot that day during an altercation between the two at the mall.

CONCLUSION

The purpose of this book is to make sure you are informed while dealing with the police. If you feel an officer is violating your rights, make a note of it. If at all possible, comply from that point on, to ensure your day in court. A police officer is the lowest form of the law. Don't give an officer the opportunity to be the judge, jury, or executioner, due to your actions. Don't allow blinding emotions to impede the process of reasoning!

Avoid being confrontational, argumen-tative, or combative. Be open minded and courteous during a traffic stop, and don't assume every stop is going to end badly. Remember, every officer interviewed said, the #1 thing you can do is comply. As stated by the 10 year veteran and echoed by all officers interviewed, having a good attitude goes a long way.

Although I suggest for you to be nice and polite, I also want you to be informed of your ability to exercise your rights. With that said, police officers have the **toughest job** in America, and for the majority, the mission is to get home to their families safely.

Hopefully, this book helps to ensure everyone makes it home.

SOURCES

Maryland State Law Library; http://lawlib.
state.md.us
CNN; https://www.cnn.com/
Cornell Law School/Legal Information
Institute; https://www.law.cornell.edu
ABC7/WJLA; https://wjla.com/
Miranda Rights; http://www.mirandarights.
org
The Baltimore Sun; https://www.baltimore-
sun.com/news
Metropolitan Police Department; https://
mpdc.dc.gov
Maryland State Law Library; https://www.
lawlib.state.md.us
Virginia Law; https://law.lis.virginia.gov/
vacode/

Library of Congress; https://www.loc.gov/law/

The Washington Post: https://www.washingtonpost.com/

U.S. News and World Report; https://www.usnews.com/news/healthiest-communities/articles/2018-10-01/new-gun-control-laws-taking-effect-in-maryland

Maryland Attorney General; http://www.marylandattorneygeneral.gov/Pages/CPD/landlords.aspx#eviction

AP News; http://www.apnews.com

The People's Law Library of Maryland; http://www.peoples-law.org

D.C. Specific Laws on Firearms and Self Defense Course

ABOUT THE AUTHOR

Born and raised in the Gum Springs Community of Alexandria, VA. Syndicated radio personality, community activist, and writer, Ken Redfearn, grew up in the streets of the District of Columbia, Maryland, and Virginia (DMV). He is driven and influenced by police injustice, and the killings of so many in our black communities across the country. He strives to educate everyone with the information needed to properly handle an encounter with the police, as a driver, passenger, pedestrian, or homeowner. Mr. Redfearn uses the perspectives of several law enforcement officers and his street knowledge in the book, "Body Armor".